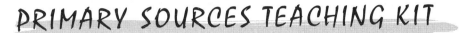

PRIMARY SOURCES TEACHING KIT

Colonial America

In *Adam's* Fall
We finned all.

Thy Life to mend,
This *Book* attend.

The *Cat* doth play,
And after flay.

A *Dog* will bite
A Thief at Night.

An *Eagle's* Flight
Is out of Sight.

The idle *Fool*
Is whipt at School.

As runs the *Glafs*,
Man's Life doth pafs.

My *Book* and *Heart*
Shall never part.

Job feels the Rod,
Yet blefses God.

Proud *Korah's* Troop
Was fwallowed up.

The *Lion* bold
The Lamb doth hold.

The *Moon* gives Light
In Time of Night.

by Karen Baicker

SCHOLASTIC
PROFESSIONAL BOOKS

New York • Toronto • London • Auckland • Sydney
Mexico City • New Delhi • Hong Kong • Buenos Aires

for Virginia Dooley and Sarah Longhi

COVER IMAGES: Brown Brothers, Sterling, PA: Poor Richard's Almanack; **Emanuel Gottlieb Leutze, Metropolitan Museum of Art/Superstock,** Jacksonville, FL: *Washington Crossing the Delaware*; **Library of Congress:** *The New England Primer*; Engraving by Paul Revere celebrating the repeal of the Stamp Act

INTERIOR IMAGES: American Tract Society/Library of Congress: 25 (right); **Bettmann/Corbis,** 33; **Brown Brothers,** Sterling, PA: 34 (left); **Emmanuel Gottlieb Leutze, Metropolitan Museum of Art/Superstock,** Jacksonville, FL: 43; **George Beamish,** Colonial Williamsburg photograph: 21; **Harvard University Portrait Collection,** Gift of Mrs. H.P. [Sarah H] Oliver to Harvard College 1852: 25 (left); **Henry E. Huntington Library and Art Gallery,** San Marino, CA: 18; **Library of Congress:** 1, 27 [control #14001032, call #Law US Massachusetts 2.1672]; 30 [LC-MSS-12021-1]; 32, 34 (right) [LC-USZ62-049991]; 36 [RM786.B79 1730 Am Imp]; 37 [E85G2 Vol. 8]; 38 (top) [LC-USZ62-10293]; 40, 41, 42; **Massachusetts Historical Society,** Boston, MA: 23; **National Museum of Natural History,** New York, NY: 20; **North Wind Picture Archives,** Alfred, ME: 22, 29, 38 (bottom); 39 (top); 39 (bottom); **NYPL/Rare Books and Manuscripts:** 35; **Rhode Island Historical Society:** 28; **State Library of Massachusetts,** Special Collections Department, Boston, MA: 26

Excerpts pages 24 and 31 courtesy "Child Life in Colonial Days" by Alice Morse Earle (Berkshire Publishers, Stockbridge, MA, 1899).

Excerpt page 25 from "Marks of a True Conversion," *The Works of the Reverend George Whitefield*, 1771–1772, London.

Excerpt page 29 from *Witchcraft Vol. 1,* page 122, Essex County Archives, Salem.

Edited by Sean Price
Picture research by Dwayne Howard
Cover design by Norma Ortiz
Interior design and illustrations by Melinda Belter
ISBN 0-590-37847-3

Contents

INTRODUCTION

Using Primary Sources in the Classroom

The colonial period of United States history formed the foundations of our country. Introducing students to primary sources from this period helps them understand that the origins of the United States were marked with real words scratched into parchment by real people. From William Bradford's handwritten copy of the Mayflower Compact to children's schoolbooks and diaries, the primary sources in this book can bring an otherwise distant historical period to life.

Primary sources offer a wealth of other benefits to your students as well. Textbooks often present a single interpretation of events; primary sources compel the reader to supply his or her own interpretation. A thoughtful analysis of primary sources requires both basic and advanced critical thinking skills: classifying documents, determining point of view, evaluating bias, comparing and contrasting, and reading for detail.

Primary sources can also help students recognize that the artifacts of our contemporary lives—a ticket stub, a school report card, a yearbook—may one day be fodder for future historians.

One of the most important steps is to help students understand the difference between primary and secondary sources. Share the chart below to demonstrate the categories to your class.

MATERIAL	DEFINITION	EXAMPLES
Primary Sources	Documents created during or immediately following the event they describe, by people who had firsthand knowledge of the event	Letters, diaries, photographs, artifacts, newspaper articles, paintings
Secondary Sources	Documents created by people who were not present at the event they describe	History books, biographies, newspaper articles

Keep a folder handy with copies of the primary source evaluation form on page 17. Encourage students to complete this reproducible as they study each document in the book. Eventually, this kind of analysis will be automatic for your students as they encounter primary sources in their future studies.

Using the Internet to Find Primary Sources

The Internet can be an amazing tool for finding primary sources. Just remind your students that extra care has to be taken in verifying that the source is reliable. Here are a few outstanding sites for using primary sources in the classroom:

Library of Congress: **http://www.loc.gov**

National Archives and Records Administration: **http://www.nara.gov**

Internet Archive of Texts and Documents: **http://history.hanover.edu/texts.htm**

Early American: **http://earlyamerican.com**

Colonial Williamsburg: **http://www.history.org**

Ask your students to find other great sites for primary sources and create their own list. Keep a running list handy, posted near a computer terminal.

Background on Life in Colonial America (c.1607–1775)

Until about 400 years ago, little changed in North America from one year to the next. The land was inhabited by dozens of Native American tribes, whose traditions carried on through gradual adaptations. The arrival of European settlers around 1600 changed those ways of life abruptly and permanently. Our continent has been changing dramatically ever since. In fact, the changes have been so radical that your students may have trouble understanding what life was like in the colonial era. Primary sources can help.

Many of today's social issues first surfaced during colonial times. Then as now, people with vastly different backgrounds lived together. Europeans, Native Americans, and Africans forged a shared, often strained, sometimes violent coexistence. The successes and failures of that great intermingling continue to define our culture.

The first Africans entered the colonies in 1619 as indentured servants. Their arrival led to the birth of slavery in the colonies and that, too, is a legacy we still struggle with today.

Religion played a central role in the development of the United States, providing cultural cohesiveness in the early colonial period. From those first seekers of religious freedom we have inherited a respect for religion and its power. But we also have a fundamental belief in the importance of separating church and state functions. This belief is born, in part, of the witch hunts and trials of the late 1600s.

And, of course, pre–Revolutionary America provides us with a wealth of information on the relationship between a colony and the mother country. The economic needs of Britain and the colonies, as well as the political struggles of each, are apparent as one reads the documents of the time.

About This Book

The primary sources that follow offer your students the chance to experience history first-hand—with all of its vague and messy detail. Your students will encounter the words of children and adults living in colonial America and they will read from the letters and diaries of some of our country's most influential early leaders. Finally, they will understand the difficulties and great opportunities presented by living through the birth of a new nation.

Your students will benefit most from working with these documents when you help to set a context and engage them with critical viewing and thinking activities. Students can prepare for a discussion about any of the documents in this collection by studying them and completing the student reproducible Evaluate That Document! (page 17). This primary source evaluation form guides students to identify important document characteristics and pose questions prior to the class discussion. Feel free to reproduce this form as you need it.

The Teaching Notes section provides background information and teaching suggestions for each document. Reproducible pages for the activity suggestions can be found at the back of the book.

Some documents, such as the Mayflower Compact (page 26), feature text that is difficult to read. For these, as well as for lengthy documents, we have included typeset selections along with the original. This way, students can explore the text as an actual, physical document, and also understand the contents. In some cases, when original documents were not available, we have typeset the text, as in the Jamestown colonist's account of The Starving Time (page 21).

Time Line of Colonial America

(c. 1607–1775)

1607   Friendly relations develop between British Captain John Smith, leader of the Jamestown colony, and Powhatan, leader of several Algonquin Indian tribes

1609–1610   The Jamestown colony faces "the starving time;" of the 214 colonists, only 60 survive

1619   The first colonial legislature, Virginia's House of Burgesses, is established; the first Africans arrive as indentured servants

1620   Pilgrims sign the Mayflower Compact and found Plymouth colony in Massachusetts; Massasoit, leader of the Wampanoag tribe, meets the Pilgrims

1621   Massasoit signs a peace treaty with the Pilgrims

1636   The first colonial college, Harvard, is founded in Massachusetts

1660   Indentured Africans become slaves for life in Jamestown

1675–1676   Metacomet (King Philip) leads Native Americans in war against the New England colonists

1681   William Penn founds Pennsylvania

1690   The first New England primer is printed

1692   Salem witch trials and executions are conducted

1730–1740s   The Great Awakening, a series of religious revivals, takes place

1754   The Albany Plan of Union is proposed by Benjamin Franklin but rejected by the colonies

1754–1763   The French and Indian War is fought mainly between France and England with the support of Native American allies on both sides; Britain wins, gaining control of land from the Atlantic Ocean to the Mississippi River

1765   Britain's Parliament passes the Stamp Act and the Quartering Act

1766   Benjamin Franklin testifies to Parliament against the Stamp Act and Parliament repeals it

1767   Parliament passes the Townsend Acts, which tax tea and other goods

1768   British troops arrive in Boston to maintain law and order

1770   Five colonists, including one African-American man, are killed by British troops in the Boston Massacre

1773   During the Boston Tea Party, colonists protest tax on tea by dumping 342 chests of British Tea into Boston Harbor

1773   Poetry of Phillis Wheatley, a slave, is first published

  Parliament passes the Quebec Act, granting religious freedom only to Roman Catholics

1774   The First Continental Congress meets in Philadelphia

1775   The battles of Lexington and Concord are fought; the Second Continental Congress meets and names George Washington commander in chief of the American troops fighting against Great Britain

Scholastic Professional Books

TEACHING NOTES

TWO WORLDS COLLIDE

A Briefe and True Report: 1588

Use with pages 18–19.

BACKGROUND

Thomas Hariot was born in 1560 in Oxford. A true Renaissance man, Hariot was a mathematician, scientist, scholar, and writer. He helped Galileo invent the telescope.

Hariot lived in the home of Sir Walter Raleigh as a tutor of math and science to sea captains. When Raleigh set out to establish the first permanent English colony in America, he brought Hariot along to record the history of the journey.

This report is a summary of their journey and the settlement of Roanoke Island in what is now North Carolina. The Roanoke colony was the first English-speaking settlement in the New World. It failed under mysterious circumstances around 1590. Jamestown became the first successful English colony.

TEACHING SUGGESTIONS

◉ Distribute copies of Evaluate That Document! (page 17). As students analyze Hariot's report, point out that it is "directed to the Adventurers, Favourers, and Wellwillers of the action, for the inhabiting and planting there." Ask students to discuss who the intended audience is. Point out that the "intended audience" is an important consideration when analyzing a document.

◉ Draw students' attention to the ways hand-writing and type from hundreds of years ago were different from today. Point out the elongated letter *s* in *necessarie* and the different spelling as well. Ask students to look for other variations in type and spelling in this document. Have them select several sentences and rewrite them in their own words, using phrases and spellings an American today would recognize.

◉ Write these two phrases from the report on the chalkboard: *the nature and manners of the natural inhabitants; discovered by the English Colony.* Discuss with students the inherent contradiction between the natural inhabitants and the English "discovery."

◉ Read aloud with students the final pages of Hariot's report. Ask them to summarize his conclusion. Did he find what he expected in Virginia? Were things better or worse? Provide students with copies of the Colonial America Journal reproducible (page 48) to frame their writing.

◉ Students can find more information about this report as well as a full transcript and photos, at **www.people.virginia.edu/~msk5d/hariot/main.html**.

◉ Distribute the Colonial America K-W-L Sampler Chart (page 44) and ask students to fill in the first two sections, listing what they know and want to learn more about concerning life in colonial America. Throughout their study of the colonies, encourage students to revisit the chart and fill in the third and fourth sections, detailing what they've learned and what they have further questions about.

The Village of Secota: 1590

Use with page 20.

BACKGROUND

John White was a cartographer and draftsman at Roanoke, and he drew a diagram of a Native American village (the Powhatan village called Secota on the drawing) for Thomas Hariot's "Report." German engraver Theodore de Bry then made this engraving based on John White's drawing.

The engraving reveals the sophistication and order of the village. The corn is shown in three different stages of growth, revealing staggered harvesting times. There are other crops as well, including squash, pumpkins, and tobacco. The activity in the center depicts trade among other Native Americans and with Europeans. The drawing also shows places for prayer, ceremony, and burial as well as dwellings.

The legend added below was supplied in 1960 by an historian, Richard L. Morton.

TEACHING SUGGESTIONS

◉ Distribute the Evaluate That Document! reproducible. Point out to students that the drawing is from a European perspective.

To spark student interest, distribute this page without the legend (trim off the bottom of the page). Give the students the labels from the legend in random order and ask them to try to identify the letters to which they correspond.

Unfortunately, almost all of the written records and drawings from the colonial time period are from the European perspective. Ask students: *How might this drawing look different if the Powhatan had drawn their own village?* Perhaps the scale of things would have been different, reflecting their own views of what was important. The ceremonial dance and the Powhatan themselves would no doubt have looked different.

The Starving Time: 1609–1610

Use with page 21.

BACKGROUND

Founded in 1607 with the hopes of finding and exporting gold, Jamestown was the first permanent British colony in the New World. Captain John Smith was its first leader. The first seven months proved quite difficult. Of the original 214 colonists, only 60 survived disease and famine. The Powhatan offered the colonists much-needed assistance, giving them corn and bread. However, the relationship became more complex as time went on. The Powhatan became angry when the colonists did not return their generosity. Some colonists stole from them, further damaging relations.

Smith played a critical role in establishing good relations with Wahunsonacock, the Powhatan leader, and in requiring that all colonists work. However, many in the original group of colonists had come from Britain's gentry class and were unaccustomed to work; they were hoping to find easy gold.

The winter of 1609–1610 became known as "The Starving Time." Historians are uncertain exactly what caused this horrible situation. We do know that relations with the Powhatan were tense (see Wahunsonacock's 1609 speech, page 22) and the winter was harsh. Armed Powhatans laid siege to Jamestown, preventing settlers from leaving the stockaded area (the nineteenth-century painting shown above the excerpt suggests how the fort may have looked). Buildings *were burned to create warmth. Many people starved to death.*

TEACHING SUGGESTIONS

Distribute copies of Evaluate That Document! (page 17). Explain to students that this description was written by a Jamestown colonist and published in the *Generall Historie of Virginia*, by Captain John Smith. The account contains entries by many different colonists.

Tell students that word of the disaster made its way back to England, and two ships arrived in May 1610. Point out that communication was very limited then compared to now—there were no television reports or telephones. People who arrived were horrified by what they saw of Jamestown. Ask students to write a description of what these newcomers saw in a letter back to England.

There are different theories and perspectives on what caused The Starving Time. Ask students to use several sources to explore why the Powhatan may have acted they way they did. Students may want to refer to Wahunsonacock's speech on page 22.

Jamestown was a garrison/fort town. Discuss with your students what impact the wall may have had upon settler's relations with the Powhatan. Ask students how the ideas expressed in this account reflect the settlers' attitudes.

Distribute copies of Comparing the Colonies (page 45) and ask students to begin their notes on Jamestown under Virginia.

Why Should You Take by Force What You Can Have by Love?: 1609

Use with page 22.

BACKGROUND

The English colonists relied on the help of the Powhatan Confederacy. When the relationship was not reciprocated, the Powhatan leader, Wahunsonacock, made this plea for respect and cooperation. His words were copied down by Captain John Smith before he left for England— just before The Starving Time.

TEACHING SUGGESTIONS

🏵 Point out to students that Wahunsonacock posed three questions to Smith: *Why will you take by force what you may obtain by love? Why will you destroy us who supply you with food? What can you get by war?* Ask your students what these questions display about the Powhatan people's beliefs and values. What might he have been trying to achieve by confronting Smith with these questions?

🏵 Using the Evaluate That Document! form (page 17), ask students to compare and contrast this document with the journal entry from The Starving Time. Have students describe the two different perspectives. Make sure to help students with unfamiliar words such as *bruit* (rumor) and *affrighteth* (frightens).

The First Thanksgiving Proclamation: 1676

Use with page 23.

BACKGROUND

The history of Thanksgiving is rife with myth and competing claims. Accounts exist describing a feast in 1621 in Plymouth. On December 12, 1621, Edward Winslow wrote a letter describing the event:

> Our corn did prove well, and God be praised, we had a good increase of Indian corn, and our barley indifferent good, but our peas not worth the gathering, for we feared they were too late sown… Many of the Indians coming amongst us, and among the rest their greatest king Massasoit, with some ninety men, whom for three days we entertained and feasted, and they went out and killed five deer, which they brought to the plantation… And although it be not always so plentiful as it was at this time with us, yet by the goodness of God, we are so far from want that we often wish you partakers of our plenty.

This feast was not repeated the following year or made official until a proclamation was issued in 1676, in Charlestown, Massachusetts.

TEACHING SUGGESTIONS

🏵 Distribute copies of Evaluate That Document! Help students read through the transcription of the Proclamation and identify the point of view. Ask students to explore what the language reveals about the beliefs of the colonists. Have them list things that the colonists were grateful for. Contrast this list with the tone and information given in the 1621 document quoted above.

🏵 Ask students what they think the first Thanksgiving spread would have consisted of. Compare that with their own Thanksgiving feasts. A good picture-supported resource students might use is *Giving Thanks: The 1621 Harvest Feast* by Kate Waters (Scholastic, 2001).

RELIGION IN THE COLONIES

Diary of Mary Osgood Sumner as a Child: late 1700s

Use with page 24.

BACKGROUND

It was common for colonial children to keep journals or monitors. These pages from a child's monitor show how religious ideals ran through every fiber of daily life. The child Mary divided her monitor so that the left page was, as she called it, her black leaf, and the right page, her white leaf. On the left page she recorded every mistake or sin she committed during the day, while on the white page she listed the good and dutiful things she had done.

TEACHING SUGGESTIONS

🏵 Distribute the Evaluate That Document! form. Explain to students that when they analyze primary source documents, they may encounter words that are no longer used today, or that have different meanings. Review the following terms and phrases with students so that they fully understand the monitor entries:

staise [stays]: part of women's and girls' undergarments that shaped their dresses

frock: dress

improving my time: both children and adults were expected to be fully occupied at all times with work or some kind of self-improvement task (reading, practicing handwriting, etc.)

parsed: learned the parts of speech

washed the butter: a step in making butter at home

sit up with: visit with, offer help to

🌼 Discuss students' reactions to the girl's list of wrong-doings and good behavior. What do they find most striking?

🌼 Ask students to consider what kinds of entries they might make for their own black leaf/white leaf journal.

The Great Awakening: 1730s and 1740s

Use with page 25.

BACKGROUND

The Great Awakening was an outburst of Christian religious zeal in the early 1700s. It was highlighted by a series of revivals led by men like George Whitefield (pronounced WHIT-field), a Methodist preacher from England. Whitefield (1714–1770) was considered the greatest evangelist of his time. Evangelicals like him believed that people can be converted from a state of sin to a "new birth" through the preaching of scripture.

During the Great Awakening, Whitefield made seven tours of Colonial America. As many as 30,000 people might have attended just one of his outdoor sermons. He even used a collapsible, portable pulpit, like the one shown on page 25, to make his job easier. Other ministers, such as Jonathan Edwards of Massachusetts and Theodore J. Frelinghuysen of New Jersey also stirred believers with their preaching.

The Great Awakening began in Connecticut and spread to the southern colonies throughout the second half of the 1700s and the 1800s. The surge in religious fervor caused splits within several Christian denominations, including the Congregationalists and the Quakers.

The excerpt shown with Whitefield's portrait was taken from a sermon entitled "Marks of a True Conversion." The oil portrait was painted by Joseph Badger sometime between 1743 and 1765.

TEACHING SUGGESTIONS

🌼 Distribute copies of Evaluate That Document! (page 17) and ask students to consider the portrait and words together to learn about the evangelical movement.

🌼 Whitefield has been compared to televangelists. Ask students to compare and contrast Whitefield's style with televangelists today.

🌼 This sermon is preserved in the collection of the Library of Congress in the online exhibit, at **http://lcweb.loc.gov/exhibits/religion/rel02. html**. Ask students to find other documents from this same collection, entitled "America as a Religious Refuge." Have students explore this web site and report on their findings to the class.

GOVERNING THE COLONIES
Mayflower Compact: 1620

Use with page 26.

BACKGROUND

The Mayflower Compact was the first effective agreement for democratic self-government in North America. When the Pilgrims landed at Plymouth in 1620, they realized the need for selecting leaders and drafting laws. Each man aboard the Mayflower signed the document, pledging to abide by decisions made as a group, even if he did not agree with all aspects of these decisions. The Mayflower Compact has been called the first American constitution.

The document was first published in 1622 in Mourt's Relation: A Journal of the Pilgrims at Plymouth. *The original version has been lost. William Bradford wrote a copy of the Mayflower Compact in his* History Of Plimoth Plantation *in 1630. That is the copy shown here.*

TEACHING SUGGESTIONS

🌼 Use the Evaluate That Document! reproducible to analyze the goals the Pilgrims had when they signed the Mayflower Compact. Ask students what sorts of situations or problems they think the Pilgrims were trying to avoid by signing the compact. Could the Jamestown colonists have benefited from such a compact when they arrived in 1607?

⚜ Encourage students to paraphrase what this document says. Make sure they can identify the main goal of establishing the first British colony in this part of the world and the religious and political justifications for doing so.

⚜ Distribute the Map of the American Colonies, 1750s (page 46) and ask students to locate where the Pilgrims landed. Have them research and fill in information about the founding of the Massachusetts Bay colony on the Comparing the Colonies chart (page 45).

Capital Laws: 1672

Use with page 27.

BACKGROUND

Capital laws carry a possible death sentence for violators. This partial list of capital laws is taken from The General Laws and Liberties of the Massachusetts Colony, published in 1672. The laws demonstrate the importance of religion in the lives of the early colonists. This document, printed in Cambridge, Massachusetts, cites the Bible passages upon which each of these capital laws is based. In contrast to the Capital Laws, many civil laws the colonists adopted were based on English common law.

TEACHING SUGGESTIONS

⚜ One of the fundamental premises of our Constitution is the separation of church and state. After students have used Evaluate That Document! (page 17) to analyze the Capital Laws excerpts, brainstorm with students how the mingling of church and state affairs became problematic, as immigrants of various religions continued to arrive.

⚜ Ask students to work in small groups to develop criminal laws they might have created if they had been among the first colonists. Ask them to keep the experiences of the Jamestown colonists and the Pilgrims in mind. Compare the groups' results.

Town Meeting: 1721

Use with page 28.

BACKGROUND

Town meetings were a form of local governance strongly associated with New England. As these records from Providence, Rhode Island show, the laws passed at town meetings were often very mundane. But the meetings gave free men an opportunity to express their views about issues of the day.

TEACHING SUGGESTIONS

⚜ Distribute the Evaluate That Document! form and initiate a discussion about the town meeting record. Ask what the decisions about the wandering of geese, the maintenance of Herndens Lane, and the killing of local squirrels might show about some of the community issues the colonists faced.

⚜ Challenge students to create a Problem and Solution chart and fill it in based on their reading of page 28.

⚜ While geese and squirrels might not have been burning issues, they gave the colonists a chance to meet together and converse about the state of the colony. But who enforced such laws? Discuss how the Treasurer might have felt to be assigned the task of determining whether squirrels' heads were from his township or from somewhere else!

⚜ How might town meetings have helped lead to the American Revolution?

⚜ Have students conduct a mock town meeting about an issue affecting your school or town. Follow parlimentary procedure.

WITCH TRIALS

Trial of Mary Easty and Witches' Petition for Bail: 1692

Use with pages 29–30.

BACKGROUND

The close ties that existed between the political and religious life of the colony

were typical in the New England colonies where Puritanism was strongest—this eventually became known as the "New England Way." Only the "visible saints" (those believed to have received God's grace) were able to vote and hold public office.

While such uniformity of belief was originally cohesive and good for the life of the colony, eventually some within the church began to question the tenets of Puritanism. The dissension was seen by many as the work of the devil (with witches as his assistants) and left the Puritans feeling that they must get rid of the devil in their midst and examine what they might have done to bring the wrath of God upon their community. In a sense, their deep religiosity and joining of church and state functions led to the witch-hunt hysteria. Depositions like the one on page 29 took place all over the colonies—Salem, Massachusetts being only the most well-known site of witch trials. The drawing from 1880 depicts the 1692 trial of Giles Corey's wife.

These trials followed none of our contemporary basic rights of representation—and so, circumstantial evidence, hysteria, and cruelty prevailed.

TEACHING SUGGESTIONS

🕎 Distribute copies of Evaluate That Document! (page 17) for students to consider during a class discussion. Read the petition aloud to the students, taking breaks to explain and discuss the content. Refer them to the Capital Laws of 1672 (page 27) which list witchcraft as a crime punishable by death.

🕎 Discuss with students what they think were the likely effects in a close-knit Puritan community on those accused of witchcraft or those who testified in defense of an accused person. What social pressures might women, such as the accused widows and housewives in the petition, have felt? Can students relate this to social pressure today?

🕎 Make a Then and Now chart on the board and discuss some of the differences between trials today and then.

🕎 The document by Abigail Williams and Ann Putnam is a deposition in the trial of Mary Easty. Ask students: When the women say they saw Mary Easty choking their friend and that she also tortured them, do you think they are lying? What do their words suggest about whether they believe what they said?

DAILY LIFE IN THE COLONIES

Diary of Anna Green Winslow: 1771

Use with page 31.

BACKGROUND

Most children who kept diaries wrote of religious matters and copied the tone and content of their older relatives' writing. The diary shown here is an exception. In her journal, Anna Green Winslow wrote of her actual daily life and sometimes trivial concerns. Therefore, it has become a more valuable resource in examining the daily lives of colonial children. In this excerpt, Anna is 12 years old and living with her aunt.

TEACHING SUGGESTIONS

🕎 Distribute copies of Evaluate That Document! Discuss how the words of a child provide a different perspective than that of an adult.

🕎 Ask students: *Do Anna's concerns seem silly? What concerns might you write about in a diary?*

🕎 Note that even though this excerpt is from a diary, it is apparently addressed to her parents (as it is signed "Your ever Dutiful Daughter"). Would students ever want their parents to read their diaries? Also notice how formally she signs her name in writing addressed to her own parents. Ask students what that might reveal about child-parent relationships among the colonists.

🕎 Children often kept journals—to help record and retain new information and experiences, to practice their handwriting and writing, and to keep a record of things they had heard (sermons, speeches). Similar to the journals were the "commonplace books," kept by many adults and children, which were a record of favorite passages of books the adult or child had read. Suggest to your students that they keep a commonplace book for one week and then share their writings with the class.

The New England Primer and Hornbook:1761

Use with pages 32–33.

BACKGROUND

The New England Primer (pronounced prim' er*) was the most commonly used textbook in the United States for over a century. First printed in 1690, it was used as a reading book for children in the first grade. Some versions were still in use as late as 1900. The Primer included many religious references.*

The Primer was small in size, usually just 2 ¹/₂ by 4 inches. This was due, in part, to the cost of paper and printing.

More emphasis was placed on the formal education of boys than girls, although girls received some formal education and a thorough training in all domestic affairs. It was the boys who would go on in a trade or profession. Before students could use a primer, they first had to master a hornbook. The hornbook consisted of a sheet of paper inscribed with the alphabet and numbers, which was attached to a sturdy wooden paddle and covered by a protective, transparent sheet of horn. Children first learned their ABCs from the hornbook and then moved on to a primer.

TEACHING SUGGESTIONS

- Distribute copies of Evaluate That Document! (page 17) and discuss what this primer can reveal about education in colonial times.

- Make copies of the Alphabet Primer (page 47). Ask students to create their own ABC book with references to things in their own lives.

- Distribute the reproducible of the hornbook on page 33 and ask students to compare the printing style expected of young students to the manuscript and cursive learned today. They might practice tracing the letters to get a feel for the detail of the script.

Ben Franklin's Almanac: 1733, 1750

Use with page 34.

BACKGROUND

Benjamin Franklin's Poor Richard's Almanack, *published under his pseudonym Richard Saunders was a best-selling book that rolled household hints, weather forecasts, scientific information, cooking recipes, and wit into one easy-to-read package. First published in 1732, the Almanack became a household item, eventually selling almost 10,000 copies per year.*

TEACHING SUGGESTIONS

- Use questions from the Evaluate That Document! form to start a discussion of the Anatomical chart image. Point out that many in colonial times still believed that illnesses and physical developments were ruled by the planets.

- Have students examine an almanac today. What kind of information does it provide? Have students read more pages from copies of *Poor Richard's Almanack*. Excerpts can be found at **http://www.vt.edu/vt98/academics/books/franklin/FranklinIndex.html**. Compare and contrast the information available and the beliefs implicit in the different almanacs.

- To this day, almanac editors may attach the title *philom.* (*philomathes*) to their names as Franklin did to his pseudonym. Encourage students to find the etymological roots of *philomathes*. They should find that *philos* means *loving* and *mathes* means *to learn*. Why might this have been an appropriate title?

Hieroglyphic Bible: 1789

Use with page 35.

BACKGROUND

This page is from a book called A Curious Hieroglyphick Bible, *featuring almost five hundred woodcuts made by American artists. The publisher and printer was Isiah Thomas, who produced children's literature. Bibles such as this were used to teach the Scriptures and reading at the same time.*

TEACHING SUGGESTIONS

- Use the Evaluate That Document! form and discuss the intention of this document. It was used to teach the Scriptures as well as teaching reading. Students might contrast a first reader they might find in a first-grade public school classroom today with this colonial first reader.

- Put a sentence with rebuses (pictures or symbols that stand for words) on the board and ask students to decipher the sentence. Then ask them to read the page from the Hieroglyphic Bible—can they figure out what it says? Discuss how the colonial outlook shaped what children were taught—what lessons might a child have taken away from reading this page?

Smallpox Epidemic: 1726

Use with page 36.

BACKGROUND

Cotton Mather was a famous minister from Boston. In 1721, a smallpox epidemic broke out in the New England colonies. Mather had heard that some doctors in Turkey had developed inoculation techniques. He urged Boston doctors to use the same techniques.

Mather recommended that people be exposed to small amounts of smallpox by rubbing the pus of smallpox victims into tiny cuts. He convinced one doctor, Zabdiel Boylston, to experiment with this treatment. Mather suffered many attacks for his controversial position, including having a bomb thrown at his home.

The experiment worked, however. Immunizations today are based on the same principle, that exposure can build immunity. The pamphlet shown (written by Boylston) was printed in London in 1726.

TEACHING SUGGESTIONS

🏵 Read aloud the following quotation from Cotton Mather's journal about the epidemic and about people's reactions to the inoculation effort:

The grievous Calamity of the Small-Pox has now entered the Town. The Practice of conveying and suffering the Small-pox by Inoculation, has never been used in America, nor indeed in our Nation, But how many Lives might be saved by it if it were practised?…
They rave, they rail, they blaspheme; they talk not only like Ideots but also like Franticks, And not only the Physician who began the Experiment, but I also am an Object of their Fury.

🏵 Many people were terrified of the new procedure and were openly hostile to Mather's support for inoculations. Discuss Mather's dilemma. What would students do if they thought they could help people with a medical treatment that many saw as threatening?

🏵 Discuss the use of the term "historical account." The account is certainly historical now, because it was published over 275 years ago. Why might Boylston have considered it historical then?

🏵 Although smallpox was eradicated in the twentieth century by vaccine, samples remain in laboratories for research and military purposes. There has been discussion recently about reintroducing the vaccine to prevent a military or terrorist reintroduction of the disease. Help students draw parallels with these recent issues.

SLAVERY

A Narrative of the Uncommon Sufferings And Surprising Deliverance: 1760

Use with page 37.

BACKGROUND

The book shown is the first independently printed slave narrative in the colonies. Briton Hammon recounts his experiences when away from his master. His adventures include being taken captive by Native Americans and by pirates as well as by the British.

About six thousand slave narratives exist from the eighteenth century, providing a unique perspective on the lives of enslaved people in colonial America. Some of them were published by abolitionist editors; some were compiled by testimonial during the Works Progress Administration's Federal Writer's Project in the 1930s, and some were published for the slave or former slave authors.

TEACHING SUGGESTIONS

🏵 Read aloud the paragraph following "CONTAINING" on the page shown. Hammon's adventures seem exaggerated. Use the Evaluate That Document! form (page 17) and encourage students to discuss whether the account is real or at least partly invented. What can they learn about Briton Hammon's perspective from that first page?

⚜ Hammon refers to General Winslow as his "good old Master." What might this say about his relationship with Winslow? Point out that the readers of these narratives were generally literate whites.

⚜ Read the excerpt from the narrative together. Discuss the fact that "captivity tales" such as this became a popular genre of slave narratives.

Runaway Slaves and Slave Auction: 1744, 1763

Use with page 38.

BACKGROUND

One indication of the miserable situations to which slaves were subjected was the posting of slave runaway notices in local papers. Some slaves were able to make it to the North, where they might pass as freemen. Often, however, they were captured and returned to their masters, who usually ordered severe punishment before returning them to their work. In the South, Native Americans came to be used as bounty hunters, although there are also many instances of Native Americans being captured and sold into slavery within the colonies and in the West Indies. This 1744 ad comes from a Charleston, South Carolina newspaper.

The slave auction notice, also shown on this page, was printed around 1763. Notices such as these are a stark reminder of how enslaved Africans were treated as property.

TEACHING SUGGESTIONS

⚜ Use questions from Evaluate That Document! (page 17) as a springboard for discussion. Discuss the fact that the runaway notice offers not only a reward, but a threat as well. Who is threatened in the notice?

⚜ The slave was an "investment" on the part of the master—an "investment" that was intended to increase the master's wealth by virtue of the labor the slave would perform. How does this explain the references to smallpox in the slave auction notice? (Students might refer to the inoculation notice on page 36).

ROOTS OF THE REVOLUTION

The Stamp Act: 1765

Use with page 39.

BACKGROUND

Between 1765 and 1770 the British Parliament passed a number of acts that steadily increased colonial mistrust and anger within the colonies. Often these acts were intended to redirect colonial purchases to the benefit of English merchants. But the colonists' protests and boycotts were so effective that Parliament repealed many of the acts.

The Stamp Act was the first direct tax and affected all paper in the colonies. For every document, letter, newspaper, and license, paper embossed with the correct stamp had to be purchased from the stamp tax office. Lawyers and newspapers were especially hard hit by this tax because of the quantity of paper they used. The Act provoked such hostility that it had a unifying effect on the colonists. The poor and the wealthy were equally opposed to this tax. "Sons of Liberty" protest groups sprang up in almost every town.

The political cartoon (bottom right) was printed on newspapers to mark the place where the stamp was to be affixed. It shows the depth of colonial hatred for the Stamp Act. A British stamp (top left) is featured for contrast.

TEACHING SUGGESTIONS

⚜ Distribute copies of Evaluate That Document! and ask students to discuss what point of view the cartoon is expressing. Ask, *What might the skull symbolize? Why did the Stamp Act anger the colonists so much? Do you think taxation is justified? If so, under what circumstances?*

⚜ Ask students to create their own political cartoon protesting the Stamp Act.

Join, or Die: 1754

Use with page 40.

BACKGROUND

Benjamin Franklin first inked this political cartoon as a message to the colonies during the French and Indian War. It later became the symbol of unity among the colonies and was reprinted frequently.

Each portion of the snake represents a colony. The cartoon later spawned the motto, "Don't Tread on Me."

TEACHING SUGGESTIONS

🌀 Ask students to identify the colonies represented on the snake. (*South Carolina, North Carolina, Virginia, Maryland, Rhode Island, New Jersey, New York, and New England*)

🌀 Ask students to interpret the message, "Join, or Die." Why did it resonate for the colonies from the time Franklin created it in 1754, through the Revolution and beyond?

Paul Revere's Obelisk: 1766

Use with page 41.

BACKGROUND

The Stamp Act was repealed in 1766. Paul Revere helped design an obelisk to celebrate the success of the repeal of the Stamp Act. Obelisks were made with oiled paper stretched over wooden frames. They were illuminated from within by candles. Hours after Revere's obelisk was erected, it was accidentally destroyed by fire. Fortunately, Revere had made an engraving of the obelisk before the fire. The engraving, shown here, is a record of the obelisk custom and art form, as well as a revolutionary account.

TEACHING SUGGESTIONS

🌀 Although it is difficult to read all the words, point out the words spelled in all capitals. Have students make a list of them and discuss why these terms may have been significant to the designers of the monument.

🌀 Have students trace the shape of one panel of the obelisk as a template. Then ask them to work in small groups to design an obelisk to commemorate an event of their choice.

News of an American Victory at Trenton: 1776

Washington Crossing the Delaware: 1851

Use with pages 42–43.

BACKGROUND

These two documents—the broadside and the painting—are paired here to help students explore the difference between a primary and a secondary source. A broadside was an announcement posted in public places. It was made from one large piece of paper and printed on one "broad side." As the broadside describes, Washington's decision to cross the Delaware took the British by surprise—in part because he and his troops made the crossing during the night and at Christmas. The well-known painting of the event, painted by Emanuel Leutze in 1851, includes several errors. For instance, it shows Washington dramatically standing up in the boat. In fact, he crossed sitting down. Also, the painting depicts the night crossing as a daytime event. And the painting shows Washington's boat painted with the stars-and-stripes flag. That flag was not adopted by the colonies until 1777, many months after Washington's crossing.

TEACHING SUGGESTIONS

🌀 Use the document (the primary source) and the painting (a secondary source) to discuss the differences between primary and secondary sources. What are the values of using each to gain insights into history? What are the drawbacks of relying on only one or the other?

🌀 Note that the broadside indicates its source in the heading at the top as "an officer of distinction in the army." Ask students how they might view headline news from today if it came from an anonymous reference. Discuss how sources are used in articles and other news-based media today. Why is it important to determine the source of information in an article?

🌀 Help students identify some of the errors in the painting, and discuss the way secondary sources can often introduce errors or myths into our understanding of history. What might it say about the perspective of Americans in 1851 reflecting back on their first commander-in-chief?

Evaluate That Document!

Title or name of document _____

Date of document _____

Type of document:

❑ letter   ❑ patent

❑ diary/journal   ❑ poster

❑ newspaper article   ❑ advertisement

❑ photograph   ❑ drawing/painting

❑ map   ❑ cartoon

❑ telegram   ❑ other _____

Point of view:

Who created this document? _____

For whom was this document created? _____

_____

What was the purpose for creating this document? _____

_____

What might the person who created it have been trying to express? _____

_____

What are two things you can learn about the time period from this primary source?

_____

_____

What questions do you have about this source?

_____

_____

_____

_____

_____

A Briefe and True Report

1588

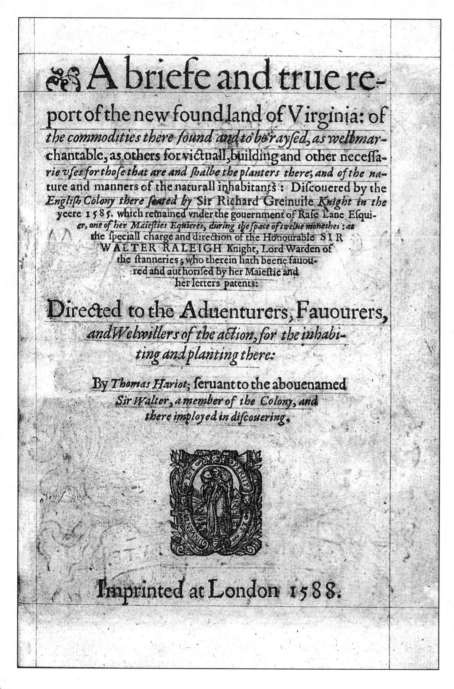

The Conclusion.

Now I haue as I hope made relation not of so fewe and smal things but that the countrey of men that are indifferent & wel disposed maie be sufficiently liked: If there were no more knowen then I haue mentioned, which doubtlesse and in great reason is nothing to that which remaineth to bee discouered, neither the soile, nor commodities. As we haue reason so to gather by the differêce we found in our trauails; for although all which I haue before spokê of, haue bin discouered & experiemented not far frõ the sea coast where was our abode & most of our trauailing: yet somtimes as we made our iourneies farther into the maine and countrey; we found the soyle to bee fatter; the trees greater and to growe thinner; the grounde more firme and deeper mould; more and larger champions; finer grasse and as good as euer we saw any in England; in some places rockie and farre more high and hillie ground; more plentie of their fruites; more abundance of beastes; the more inhabited with people, and of greater pollicie & larger dominions, with greater townes and houses.

*W*hy may wee not then looke for in good hope from the inner parts of more and greater plentie, as well of other things, as of those which wee haue alreadie discouered? Vnto the Spaniardes happened the like in discouering the maine of the West Indies. The maine also of this countrey of Virginia, extending some wayes so many hundreds of leagues, as otherwise then by the relation of the inhabitants wee haue most certaine knowledge of, where yet no Christian Prince hath any possession or dealing, cannot but yeeld many kinds of excellent commodities, which we in our discouerie haue not yet seene . . . .

*F*or the holsomnesse thereof I neede to say but thus much: that for all the want of prouision, as first of English victuall; excepting for twentie daies, wee liued only by drinking water and by the victuall of the countrey, of which some sorts were very straunge vnto vs, and might haue bene thought to haue altered our temperatures in such sort as to haue brought vs into some greeuous and dangerous diseases: secõdly the want of English meanes, for the taking of beastes, fishe, and foule, which by the helpe only of the inhabitants and their meanes, coulde not bee so suddenly and easily prouided for vs, nor in so great numbers & quantities, nor of that choise as otherwise might haue bene to our better satisfaction and contentment. Some want also wee had of clothes. Furthermore, in all our trauailes which were most speciall and often in the time of winter, our lodging was in the open aire vpon the grounde. And yet I say for all this, there were but foure of our whole company (being one hundred and eight) that died all the yeere and that but at the latter ende thereof and vpon none of the aforesaide causes. For all foure especially three were feeble, weake, and sickly persons before euer they came thither, and those that knewe them much marueyled that they liued so long beeing in that case, or had aduentured to trauaile. . . .

*A*nd this is all the fruites of our labours, that I haue thought necessary to aduertise you of at this present: what els concerneth the nature and manners of the inhabitants of Virginia: The number with the particularities of the voyages thither made; and of the actions of such that haue bene by Sir Walter Raleigh therein and there imployed, many worthy to bee remembered. . . . This referring my relation to your fauourable constructions, expecting good successe of the action, from him which is to be acknowledged the authour and gouernour not only of this but of all things els, I take my leaue of you, this moneth of February. 1588.

FINIS

Excerpt from *A Briefe and True Report...* by Thomas Hariot, 1588

The Village of Secota

1590

National Museum of Natural History

A – Tomb of chieftains
B – Place of assembly for prayer
C – Ceremonial dance
D – Feast
E – Tobacco
F – Watchman guarding corn

G – Green corn, between rows of ripe corn
H – Squash
I – Pumpkins
K – Ceremonial fire
L – Body of water

Scholastic Professional Books

The Starving Time

1609–1610

George Beamish

Now we all found the losse of Captaine *Smith*, yea his greatest maligners could now curse his losse: as for corne provision and contribution from the Salvages, we had nothing but mortall wounds, with clubs and arrowes; as for our Hogs, Hens, Goats, Sheepe, Horse, or what lived, our commanders, officers and Salvages daily consumed them, some small proportions sometimes we tasted, till all was devoured; then swords, armes, pieces, or any thing, wee traded with the Salvages, whose cruell fingers were so oft imbrewed in our blouds, that what by their crueltie, our Governours indiscretion, and the losse of our ships, of five hundred within six moneths after Captaine *Smiths* departure [October 1609–March 1610], there remained not past sixtie men, women and children, most miserable and poore creatures; and those were preserved for the most part, by roots, herbes, acornes, walnuts, berries, now and then a little fish: they that had startch in these extremities, made no small use of it; yea even the very skinnes of our horses.

Nay, so great was our famine, that a Salvage we slew and buried, the poorer sort tooke him up againe and eat him; and so did divers one another boyled and stewed with roots and herbs: And one amongst the rest did kill his wife, powdered [i.e., salted] her, and had eaten part of her before it was knowne; for which hee was executed, as hee well deserved: now whether shee was better roasted, boyled or carbonado'd [i.e., grilled], I know not; but of such a dish as powdered wife I never heard of.

This was the time, which still to this day we called the starving time; it were too vile to say, and scarce to be beleeved, what we endured. . .

A Jamestown colonist's account,
from *Generall Historie of Virginia*, by Captain John Smith, 1624

Scholastic Professional Books

"Why Should You Take by Force What You Can Have by Love?"

1609

Captaine Smith, you may understand that I having seene the death of all my people thrice, and not any one living of these three generations but my selfe; I know the difference of Peace and Warre better than any in my Country. But now I am old, and ere long must die; my brothers, Opitchapam, Opechancanough, and Kekataugh, my two sisters, and their two daughters, are distinctly each others successors. I wish their experience no lesse then mine, and your love to them no lesse than mine to you.

But this bruit from Nandsamund, that you are come to destroy my Country, so much affrighteth all my people as they dare not visit you. What will it availe you to take that by force you may quickly have by love, or to destroy them that provide you food. What can you get by warre, when we can hide our provisions and fly to the woods? Whereby you must famish by wronging us your friends. And why are you thus jealous of our loves seeing us unarmed, and both doe, and are willing still to feede you, with that you cannot get but by our labours? Think you I am so simple, not to know it is better to eate good meate, lye well, and sleepe quietly with my women and children, laugh and be merry with you, have copper, hatchets, or what I want being your friend: then be forced to flie from all, to lie cold in the woods, feede upon Acornes, rootes, and such trash, and be so hunted by you, that I can neither rest, eate, nor sleepe; but my tyred men must watch, and if a twig but breake, every one cryeth there commeth Captaine Smith: then must I fly I know not whether: and thus with miserable feare, end my miserable life, leaving my pleasures to such youths as you, which through your rash unadvisednesse may quickly as miserably end, for want of that, you never know where to finde. Let this therefore assure you of our loves, and every yeare our friendly trade shall furnish you with Corne; and now also, if you would come in friendly manner to see us, and not thus with your guns and swords as to invade your foes.

POWHATAN
Held this state & fashion when Capt. Smith
was delivered to him prisoner
1607

North Wind Picture Archives

Wahunsonacock ("Powhatan"), 1609

Scholastic Professional Books

The First Thanksgiving Proclamation

1676

The holy God having by a long and Continued Series of his Afflictive dispensations in and by the present Warr with the Heathen Natives of this Land, written and brought to pass bitter things against his own Covenant people in this wilderness, yet so that we evidently discern that in the midst of his judgements he hath remembred mercy, having remembred his Footstool in the day of his sore displeasure against us for our sins, with many singular Intimations of his Fatherly Compassion, and regard: reserving many of our Towns from Desolation Threatned, and attempted by the Enemy, and giving us especially of late with our Confederates many signal Advantages against them, without such Disadvantage to our selves as formerly we have been sensible of, if it be of the Lords mercies that we are not consumed, It certainly bespeaks our positive Thankfulness, when our Enemies are in any measure disappointed or destroyed: and fearing the Lord should take notice under so many Intimations of his returning mercy, we should be found an Insensible people, as not standing before him with Thanksgiving, as well as lading him with our Complaints in the time of pressing Afflictions:

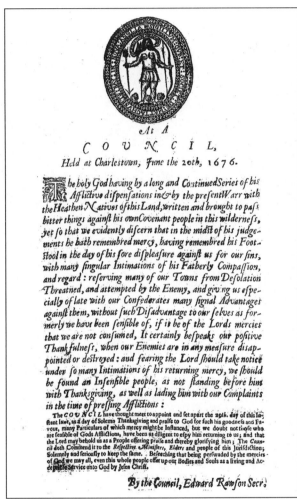

Massachusetts Historical Society

The COUNCIL have thought meet to appoint and set apart the 29th day of this instant *June*, as a day of Solemn Thanksgiving and praise to God for such his goodness and Favour, many Particulars of which mercy might be Instanced, but we doubt not those who are sensible of Gods Afflictions, have been as diligent to espy him returning to us; and that the Lord may behold us as a People offering praise and thereby glorifying him; the *Council* doth Commend it to the *Respective Ministers, Elders* and people of this Jurisdiction; Solemnly and seriously to keep the same. Beseeching that being perswaded by the mercies of God we may all, even this whole people offer up our Bodies and Souls as a living and Acceptable Service unto God by Jesus Christ.

By the Council, Edward Rawson Secr.

Scholastic Professional Books

Diary of Mary Osgood Sumner as a Child

late 1700s

Earle, *Child Life in Colonial Days*

Scholastic Professional Books

The Great Awakening

1730s and 1740s

George Whitefield

American Tract Society / Library of Congress

...The Lord Jesus Christ knew this full well; he knew how desperately wicked and deceitful men's hearts were; he knew very well how many would go to hell even by the very gates of heaven, how many would climb up even to the door, and go so near as to knock at it, and yet after all be dismissed with a "verily I know you not." The Lord, therefore, plainly tells us, what great change must be wrought in us, and what must be done for us, before we can have any well grounded hopes of entering into the kingdom of heaven. Hence, he tells Nicodemus, "that unless a man be born again, and from above, and unless a man be born of water and of the Spirit, he cannot enter into the kingdom of God....

Excerpt from "Marks of a True Conversion" sermon, c. 1730s–1740s

Harvard University Portrait Collection

Scholastic Professional Books

Mayflower Compact

1620

*In ye name of god Amen. We whose names are under-writen,
the loyall subjects of our dread Soueraigne Lord King Iames
by ye grace of god, of great Britaine, franc, & Ireland king.
defendor of ye faith, &*

*Haueing under-taken, for ye glorie of god, and aduancements
of ye christian faith, and honour of our king & countrie, a voyage to
plant ye first colonie in ye Northerne parts of virginia. doe
by these presents solemnly & mutualy in ye presence of god, and
one of another, couenant, & combine our selues togeather into a
ciuill body politick; for our better ordering, & preseruation & fur=
theranc of ye ends aforesaid; and by vertue hearof to enacte,
constitute, and frame shuch just & equall Lawes, ordinances,
Acts, constitutions, & offices, from time to time, as shall be thought
most meete & convenient for ye generall good of ye colonie: vnto
which we promise all due submission and obedienc. In witnes
wherof we haue hereunder subscribed our names at cap=
codd ye ·11· of Nouember, in ye year of ye raigne of our soueraigne
Lord king James of England, franc, & Ireland ye eighteenth,
and of Scotland ye fiftie fourth, An: Dom ·1620·*

State Library of Massachusetts

*In the name of God, Amen. We whose names are underwritten, the
loyall Subjects of our dread Soveraigne Lord King James, by the grace
of God of Great Britaine, France, and Ireland King Defender of the
Faith, &c.*

*Having under-taken for the glory of God, and advancement of the
Christian Faith, and honour of our King and Countrey, a Voyage to
plant the first Colony in the Northerne parts of VIRGINIA; doe by these
presents solemnly & mutually in the presence of God and one of
another, covenant, and combine our selves together into a civill body
politicke, for our better ordering and preservation, and furtherance of
the ends aforesaid; and by vertue hereof to enact, constitute, and frame
such just and equall Lawes, Ordinances, acts, constitutions, & offices
from time to time, as shall be thought most meet and convenient for the
generall good of the Colony: unto which we promise all due submission
and obedience. In witness whereof we have hereunder subscribed our
names at Cape Cod the ·11· of November, in the yeare of the Raigne
of our Soveraigne Lord King JAMES of England, France, and Ireland,
the eighteenth and of Scotland the fifty-fourth. Anno Domino ·1620·*

Scholastic Professional Books

Trial of Mary Easty

1692

North Wind Picture Library

Abigail Williams and Ann Putnam, Jr. v. Mary Easty,
John Willard, and Mary Witheridge

The Deposistion of Abigaill williams and Ann putnam who testifieth and
saith that we both goeing along with goodman Abby and Sarah Trask the 20th
of may 1692 to the house of Constable Jno: putnam to se mercy lewes. as we ware
in the way we both saw the Apperishtion of Gooddy Estick the very same
woman that was sent whom the other day: and also the Apperishtion of Goody
Estick tould us both that now she was afflecting of Mircy lewes because she
would not clear hir as others did and w'n came to who laye speachless and in a
sad condition we saw there the Apperishtions of gooddy Estick and Jno. willard
and mary witheridge afflecting and choaking mircy lewes in a most dreadfull
maner.which did most greviously affright us and immediatly gooddy Estick did
fall upon us and tortor us allso Redy to choake us to death

Abigail Williams and An putnam Testified to the truth of the abous'd
Evedence

Salem Village May the 23d. 1692

Before us
*John Hathorne
*Jonathan. Corwin
Assists

Witches' Petition for Bail

1692

The humble petition of us whose names are subscribed hereunto now prisoners at Ipswich humbly showeth, that some of us have lyen in the prison many monthes, and some of us many weekes, who are charged with witchcraft, and not being conscious to our selves of any guilt of that nature lying upon our consciences; our earnest request is that seeing the winter is soe far come on that it can not be expected that we should be tryed during this winter season, that we may be released out of prison for the Present upon Bayle to answer what we are charged with in the Spring. For we are not in this unwilling nor afrayd to abide the tryall before any Judicature apoynted in convenient season of any crime of that nature; we hope you will put on the bowells of compassion soe far as to consider of our suffering condicion in the present state we are in, being like to perish with cold in lying longer in prison in this cold season of the yeare, some of us being aged either about or nere fourscore some though younger yet being with child, and one giving suck to a child not yet ten weekes old, and all of us weake and infirme at the best, and one fettered with irons this halfe yeare, and allmost distroyed with soe long an imprisonment. Thus hoping you will grant us a release at the present that we may be not be left to perish in this miserable condicion. We shall always pray, et.

Diary of Anna Green Winslow

1771

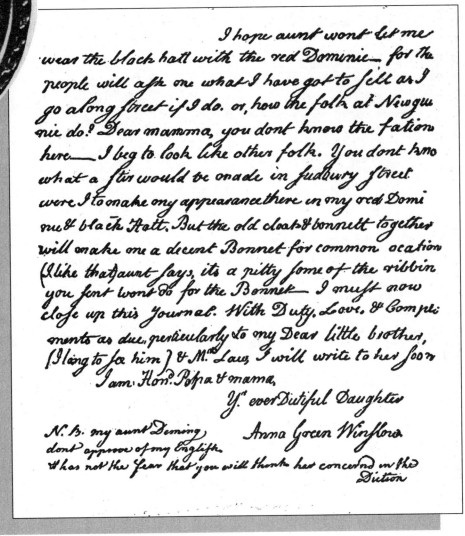

I hope aunt wont let me
wear the black hatt with the red Dominie— for the
people will ask one what I have got to sell as I
go along street if I do. or, how the folk at Newgu
nie do? Dear mamma, you dont know the fation
here—— I beg to look like other folk. You dont kmo
what a stir would be onade in sudbury street.
were I to onake ony appearance there in my red Domi
nie & black Hatt. But the old cloak & bonnett together
will onake one a decent Bonnet for common ocation
(I like that) aunt says, its a pitty some of the ribbin
you sent wont do for the Bonnet—— I must now
close up this Journal. With Duty, Love, & Compli
ments as due, perticularly to my Dear little brother,
(I long to see him) & Mrs Law, I will write to her soon
I am Honrd Papa & mama,
Yr ever Dutiful Daughter
Anna Green Winslow

N. B. my aunt Deming,
dont approve of my English.
& has not the sear that you will thinke her concerned in the
Diction

Earle, *Child Life in Colonial Days*

New England Primer

1761

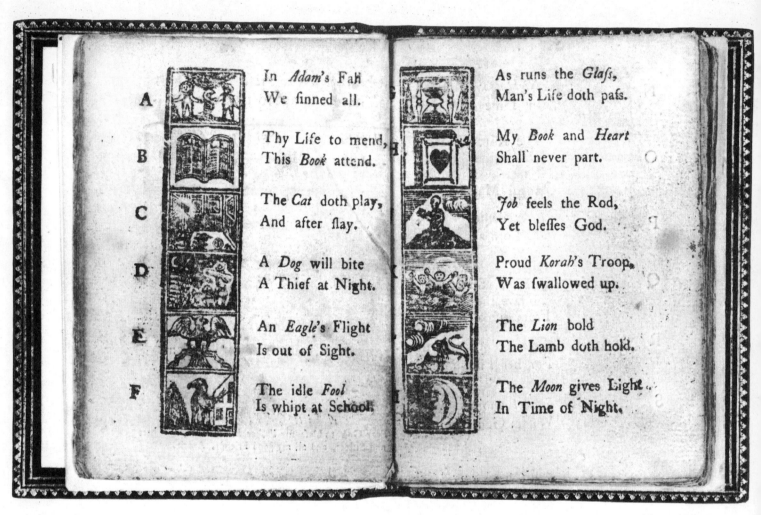

A   In *Adam's* Fall / We finned all.

B   Thy Life to mend, / This *Book* attend.

C   The *Cat* doth play, / And after flay.

D   A *Dog* will bite / A Thief at Night.

E   An *Eagle's* Flight / Is out of Sight.

F   The idle *Fool* / Is whipt at School.

G   As runs the *Glass*, / Man's Life doth pass.

H   My *Book* and *Heart* / Shall never part.

I   *Job* feels the Rod, / Yet blesses God.

K   Proud *Korah's* Troop, / Was swallowed up.

L   The *Lion* bold / The Lamb doth hold.

M   The *Moon* gives Light / In Time of Night.

Library of Congress

Scholastic Professional Books

Hornbook

1761

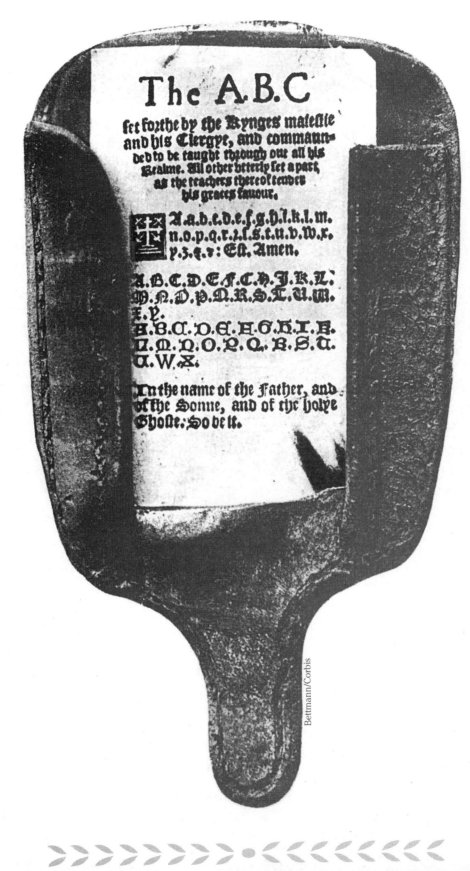

Bettmann/Corbis

Ben Franklin's Almanac

1733

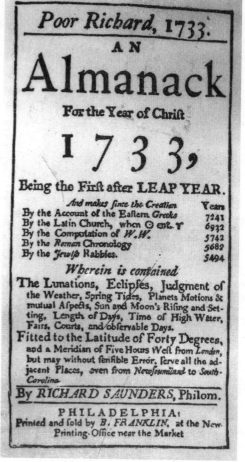

> Poor Richard, 1733.
> AN
> # Almanack
> For the Year of Chrift
> ## 1733,
> Being the Firft after LEAP YEAR.
>
> *And makes fince the Creation* Years
> By the Account of the Eaftern *Greeks* 7241
> By the Latin Church, when ☉ ent. ♈ 6932
> By the Computation of *W.W.* 5742
> By the *Roman* Chronology 5682
> By the *Jewifh* Rabbies. 5494
>
> *Wherein is contained*
> The Lunations, Eclipfes, Judgment of
> the Weather, Spring Tides, Planets Motions &
> mutual Afpects, Sun and Moon's Rifing and Set-
> ting, Length of Days, Time of High Water,
> Fairs, Courts, and obfervable Days.
> Fitted to the Latitude of Forty Degrees,
> and a Meridian of Five Hours Weft from *London*,
> but may without fenfible Error, ferve all the ad-
> jacent Places, even from *Newfoundland* to *South-
> Carolina*
> By *RICHARD SAUNDERS*, Philom.
> PHILADELPHIA:
> Printed and fold by B. FRANKLIN, at the New-
> Printing-Office near the Market

Brown Brothers

1750

The ANATOMY of Man's Body, as governed by the Twelve CONSTELLATIONS.

♈ The Head and Face.

♊ Arms — ♌ Heart — ♎ Reins — ♐ Thighs — ♒ Legs

♉ Neck — ♋ Breaft — ♍ Bowels — ♏ Secrets — ♑ Knees

♓ The Feet.

To know where the Sign is

Firft Find the Day of the Month, and againft the Day you have the Sign or place of the Moon in the 6th Column. Then finding the Sign here, it fhews the part of the Body it governs.

The Names and Characters of the Seven Planets

☉ Sol, ♄ Saturn, ♃ Jupiter, ♂ Mars, ♀ Venus, ☿ Mercury, ☽ Luna, ☊ Dragon's head, and ☋ tail.

The Five Afpects.

☌ Conjunction, ☍ Oppofition, ✶ Sextile, △ Trine, □ Quartile.

Library of Congress

Scholastic Professional Books

Hieroglyphic Bible
1789

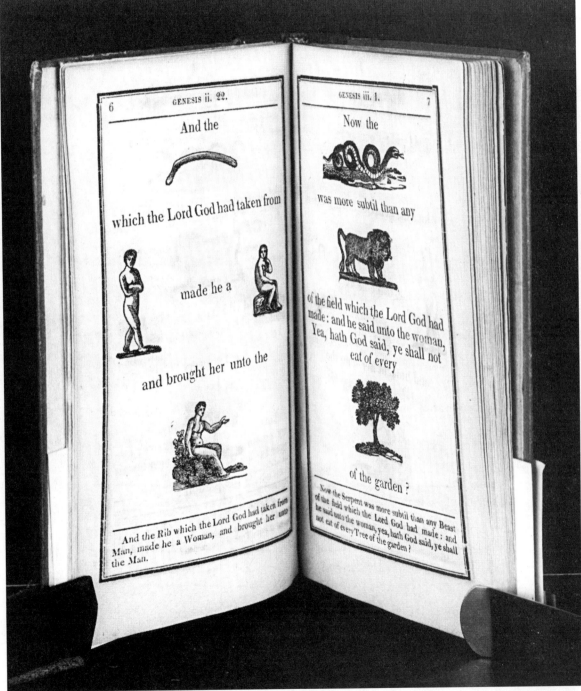

New York Public Library

Smallpox Epidemic
1726

Hiftorical ACCOUNT
OF THE
SMALL·POX
INOCULATED
IN
NEW ENGLAND,

Upon all Sorts of Perfons, *Whites*, *Blacks*, and of all Ages and Conftitutions.

With fome Account of the Nature of the Infection in the NATURAL and INOCULATED Way, and their different Effects on HUMAN BODIES.

With fome fhort DIRECTIONS to the UN-EXPERIENCED in this Method of Practice.

Humbly dedicated to her Royal Highnefs the Princefs of WALES, By *Zabdiel Boylfton*, F. R. S.

The Second Edition, Corrected.

LONDON:

Printed for S. CHANDLER, at the Crofs-Keys in the *Poultry*. M. DCC. XXVI.

Re-Printed at *BOSTON* in *N. E.* for S. GERRISH in *Cornhil*, and T. HANCOCK at the Bible and Three Crowns in *Annftreet*. M. DCC. XXX.

A Narrative of the Uncommon Sufferings

1760

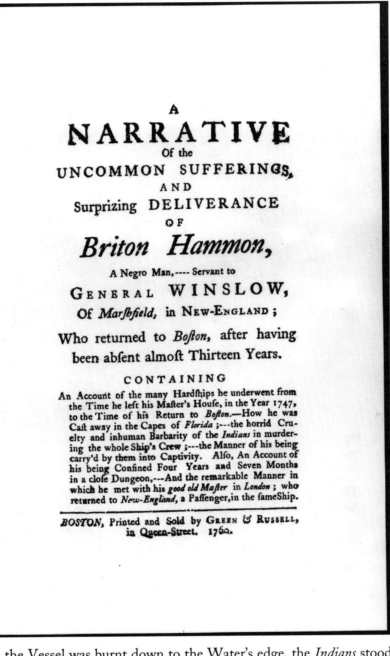

A
NARRATIVE
Of the
UNCOMMON SUFFERINGS,
AND
Surprizing DELIVERANCE
OF
Briton Hammon,
A Negro Man, ---- Servant to
GENERAL WINSLOW,
Of *Marshfield,* in NEW-ENGLAND;

Who returned to *Boston,* after having been abfent almoft Thirteen Years.

CONTAINING

An Account of the many Hardfhips he underwent from the Time he left his Mafter's Houfe, in the Year 1747, to the Time of his Return to *Boston.*——How he was Caft away in the Capes of *Florida* ;---the horrid Cruelty and inhuman Barbarity of the *Indians* in murdering the whole Ship's Crew ;---the Manner of his being carry'd by them into Captivity. Alfo, An Account of his being Confined Four Years and Seven Months in a clofe Dungeon,----And the remarkable Manner in which he met with his *good old Mafter* in *London* ; who returned to *New-England,* a Paffenger, in the fameShip.

BOSTON, Printed and Sold by GREEN & RUSSELL, in Queen-Street. 1760.

Library of Congress

As soon as the Vessel was burnt down to the Water's edge, the *Indians* stood for the Shore, together with our Boat, on board of which they put 5 hands. After we came to the Shore, they led me to their Hutts, where I expected notheing but immediate Death, and as they spoke broken English, were often telling me, while coming from the Sloop to the Shore, that they intended to roast me alive. But the Providence of God ordere'd it otherways, for He appeared for my Help, *in this Mount of Difficulty,* and they were better to me than my Fears, and soon unbound me, but set a Guard over me every Night.

An excerpt from Hammon's book

Runaway Slaves and Slave Auction

1744

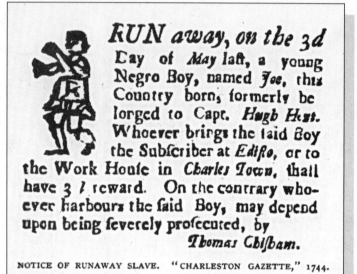

RUN away, on the 3d Day of May laſt, a young Negro Boy, named Joe, this Country born, formerly belonged to Capt. Hugh Heſt. Whoever brings the ſaid Boy the Subſcriber at Ediſto, or to the Work Houſe in Charles Town, ſhall have 3 *l* reward. On the contrary whoever harbours the ſaid Boy, may depend upon being ſeverely proſecuted, by

Thomas Chiſham.

NOTICE OF RUNAWAY SLAVE. "CHARLESTON GAZETTE," 1744.

North Wind Picture Library

1763

TO BE SOLD on board the Ship Bance-Iſland, on tueſday the 6th of May next, at Aſhley-Ferry; a choice cargo of about 250 fine healthy

NEGROES,

juſt arrived from the Windward & Rice Coaſt. —The utmoſt care has already been taken, and ſhall be continued, to keep them free from the leaſt danger of being infected with the SMALL-POX, no boat having been on board, and all other communication with people from Charles-Town prevented.

Auſtin, Laurens, & Appleby.

N. B. Full one Half of the above Negroes have had the SMALL-POX in their own Country.

Library of Congress

The Stamp Act

1765

Join, or Die

1754

Scholastic Professional Books

Paul Revere's Obelisk

1766

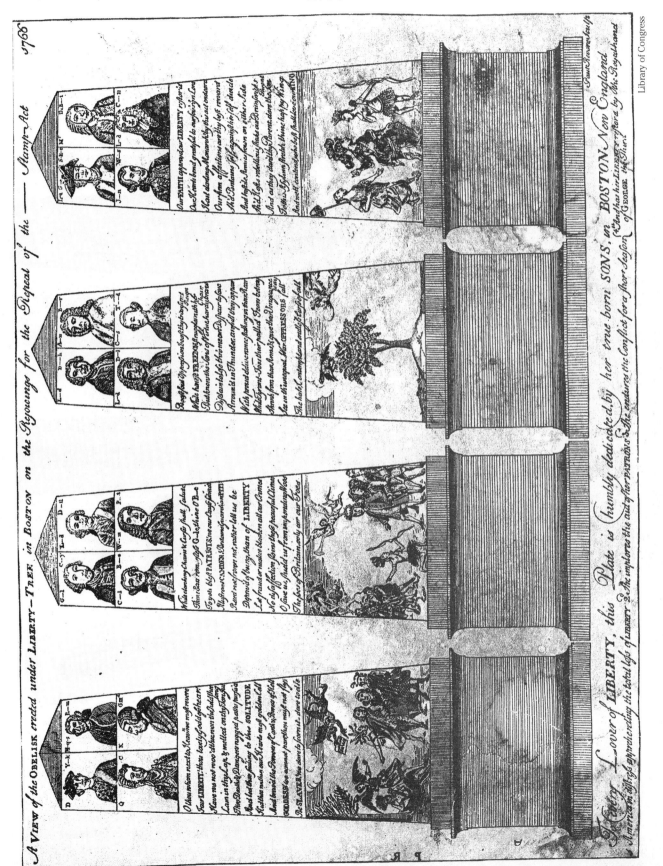

News of an American Victory at Trenton

1776

BALTIMORE, December 30.

CONGRESS received the following Intelligence from the Council of Safety, as coming from " an Officer of distinction in the Army."

Head Quarters, Newtown, Bucks county, Dec. 27.

IT was determined some days ago, that our army should pass over to Jersey at three different places and attack the enemy, accordingly about 2,500 men and 20 brass field pieces with his Excellency General Washington at their head, and Major General Sullivan and General Green in command of two divisions passed over on the night of Christmas, and about three o'Clock A. M. were on their march by two routs towards Trenton—The night was sleety and cold and the roads slippery, that it was day break when we were two miles from Trenton, but happily the enemy were not apprized of our design, and our advance party were on their guards at half a mile from town where General Sullivan and General Green's divisions soon came into the same road.

Their guard gave our advance party several smart fires as we drove them, but we soon got two field pieces at play and several others in a small time, and one of our columns pushing down on the right while the other advanced on the left into the town. The enemy consisting of about 1500 Hessians under Col. Rohl formed and made some smart fires from their musquetry and 6 field pieces, but our people pressed from every quarter and drove them from their cannon—They retired towards a field behind a piece of woods up the creek from Trenton and formed in two bodies, which I expected would have brought on a smart action from our troops who had formed very near them, but at that instant as I came in full view of them from the back of the woods with his Excellency General Washington, an officer informed him that one party had grounded their arms and surrendered prisoners—The other soon followed their example except a part which had got off in the hazy weather towards Princeton; their light horse made off on our first approach—Too much praise cannot be given to the officers and men of every regiment, who seemed to vie with each other, and by their active spirited behaviour, they soon put an honorable issue to this glorious day.

You may rejoice and be exceeding glad at this intelligence of our success, which I hope and believe will prevent the enemy from passing the river.

We took three standards, 6 fine brass cannon and near 1000 stand of arms. They must have had about 20 or 30 killed.

" I was immediately sent off with the prisoners to M'Conkey's ferry, and have got about seven hundred and fifty safe in town and a few miles from here, on this side the ferry, viz. one Lieutenant Colonel, two Majors, four Captains, seven Lieutenants, and eight Ensigns. We left Col. Rohl, the Commandant, wounded, on his parole, and several other officers and wounded men at Trenton. We lost but two of our men that I can hear of, a few wounded, and one brave officer, Capt. Washington, who assisted in securing their artillery, shot in in both hands. Indeed every officer and private behaved well, and it was a fortunate day to our arms, which I the more rejoice at, having an active part in it. The success of this day will greatly animate our friends, and add fresh courage to our new army, which, when formed, will be sufficient to secure us from the depredations or insults of our enemy.

——" Gen. Ewing's division could not pass at Trenton for the ice, which also impeded Gen. Cadwalader passing over with all his cannon and the militia, though part of his troops were over, and if the whole could have passed, we should have swept the coast to Philadelphia.

Published by order of Congress.

CHARLES THOMSON, Sec'ry.

BALTIMORE: Printed by JOHN DUNLAP.

Washington Crossing the Delaware

1851

Metropolitan Museum of Art / Superstock

Washington Crossing the Delaware, 1851
by Emanuel Gottlieb Leutze

KWL Sampler Chart

In the sampler below, write down what you already know about life in colonial America in the *K* section, and then what you want to learn in the *W* section. When you've found the answers to your questions, record your discoveries in the *L* section and new questions in the *What I Still Want to Learn* section.

What I Know
K
_____
_____
_____
_____
_____

What I Want to Know
W
_____
_____
_____
_____
_____

What I Learned
L
_____
_____
_____
_____
_____

What I Still Want to Learn

_____   _____
_____   _____
_____   _____

name _____ aged _____, date _____

Scholastic Professional Books

Name _____ Date _____

>>>>>>>>>> • <<<<<<<<<<

Comparing the Colonies

Show what you know about the founding of each of the original 13 colonies. Be sure to fill in the date the colony was established, where the European settlers came from, why they came to that location, and what Native American groups were already there.

Connecticut   founding leader: _____ est.: _____

_____

_____

_____

Delaware   founding leader: _____ est.: _____

_____

_____

_____

Georgia   founding leader: _____ est.: _____

_____

_____

_____

Maryland   founding leader: _____ est.: _____

_____

_____

_____

Massachusetts   founding leader: _____ est.: _____

_____

_____

_____

New Hampshire founding leader: _____ est.: _____

_____

_____

_____

New Jersey   founding leader: _____ est.: _____

_____

_____

New York   founding leader: _____ est.: _____

_____

_____

_____

North Carolina founding leader: _____ est.: _____

_____

_____

_____

Pennsylvania founding leader: _____ est.: _____

_____

_____

_____

Rhode Island founding leader: _____ est.: _____

_____

_____

_____

South Carolina founding leader: _____ est.: _____

_____

_____

_____

Virginia   founding leader: _____ est.: _____

_____

_____

_____

>>>>>>>>>> • <<<<<<<<<<

Map of the American Colonies, 1750s

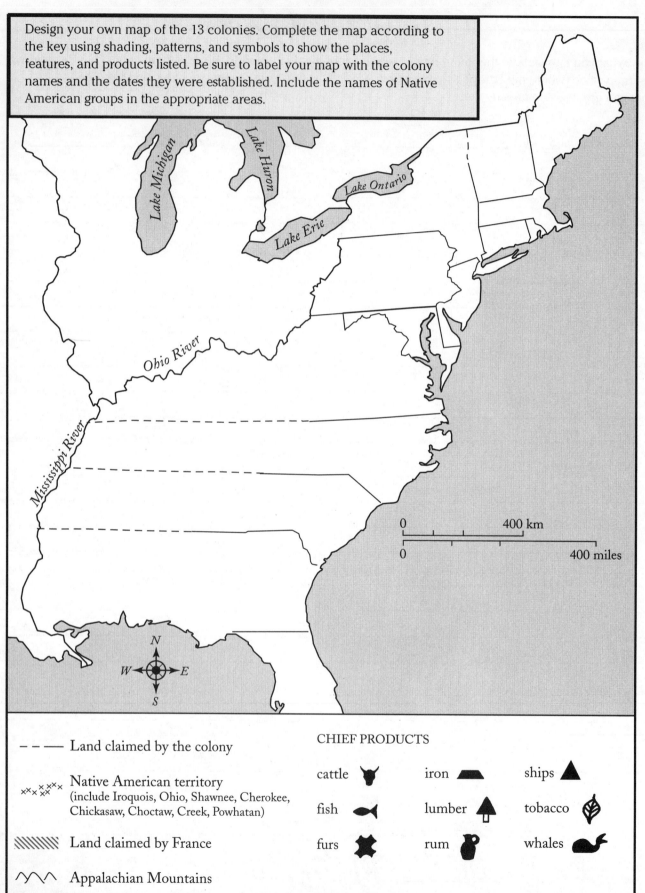

Design your own map of the 13 colonies. Complete the map according to the key using shading, patterns, and symbols to show the places, features, and products listed. Be sure to label your map with the colony names and the dates they were established. Include the names of Native American groups in the appropriate areas.

Lake Michigan

Lake Huron

Lake Ontario

Lake Erie

Ohio River

Mississippi River

0   400 km

0   400 miles

N
W   E
S

– – – — Land claimed by the colony

××××× Native American territory
(include Iroquois, Ohio, Shawnee, Cherokee, Chickasaw, Choctaw, Creek, Powhatan)

\\\\\\ Land claimed by France

∧∧∧∧ Appalachian Mountains

CHIEF PRODUCTS

cattle

fish

furs

iron

lumber

rum

ships

tobacco

whales

Alphabet Primer

After they studied with a hornbook, many students in colonial times used small printed books called primers, such as the one shown on page 32. Create your own alphabet primer below. Make sure you have three copies of this page to make enough letter blocks for a full alphabet. Create an image for each letter (such as apple for A) and write a short saying or rhyming note for each. Use the colonial-style cursive alphabet below as a model, or create your own script for each letter. Cut the finished squares out and paste them on pages that you can staple together to create a full primer. (You might want to work with a partner or in a group to complete this project.)

A
a   An apple a
day keeps the
doctor away.

Aa Bb Cc Dd Ee Ff Gg Hh Ii Jj Kk Ll Mm
Nn Oo Pp Qq Rr Ss Tt Uu Vv Ww Xx Yy Zz

Name _____ Date _____

Colonial America Journal

Scholastic Professional Books